Animal Spikes and Spines

Teeth

Rebecca Rissman

Heinemann Library
Chicago, Illinois

www.capstonepub.com
Visit our website to find out
more information about
Heinemann-Raintree books.

To order:
☎ Phone 800-747-4992
⌨ Visit www.capstonepub.com
to browse our catalog and order online.

© 2011 Heinemann Library
an imprint of Capstone Global Library, LLC
Chicago, Illinois

Edited by Rebecca Rissman, Dan Nunn
    and Sian Smith
Designed by Joanna Hinton-Malivoire
Picture research by Tracy Cummins
Production by Victoria Fitzgerald
Originated by Capstone Global Library Ltd

Library of Congress Cataloging-in-Publication Data
Rissman, Rebecca.
  Teeth / Rebecca Rissman.—1st ed.
     p. cm.—(Animal spikes and spines)
  Includes bibliographical references and index.
  ISBN 978-1-4329-5042-2 (hc)—ISBN 978-1-4329-5049-1 (pb)
1. Teeth—Juvenile literature. I. Title.
  QL858.R57 2012
  591.4'4—dc22
                              2010044794

Acknowledgments
We would like to thank the following for permission to reproduce
photographs: National Geographic Stock pp **4** (Alaska Stock
Images), **5** (Beverly Joubert), **13** (Mike Parry/Minden Pictures),
14 (Paul Sutherland), **23b** (Beverly Joubert); Photolibrary pp **6**
(Megan Q Daniels), **9** & **10** (both Kurt Madersbacher), **11** &
12 (both Anup Shah), **22** (Kurt Madersbacher); Shutterstock
pp **7** (Graeme Shannon), **8** (Ecoventurestravel), **15** & **16** (both
Timothy Craig Lubcke), **20** (Eduardo Cervantes), **21** (Ben44), **23a**
(© saasemen); Superstock pp **17** & **18** (both © Pacific Stock).

Cover photograph of a hippopotamus reproduced with
permission of Shutterstock (Timothy Craig Lubcke). Back
cover photograph of a caiman reproduced with permission of
Shutterstock (Ecoventurestravel).

We would like to thank Michael Bright, Nancy Harris, Dee Reid,
and Diana Bentley for their assistance in the preparation of
this book.

Every effort has been made to contact copyright holders of
material reproduced in this book. Any omissions will be rectified in
subsequent printings if notice is given to the publisher.

Contents

Animal Body Parts

Animals have different body parts.

teeth

Some animals have teeth.

What Are Teeth?

Teeth are hard body parts.

Teeth grow in animals' mouths.

Teeth come in many shapes
and sizes.

Different Teeth

Teeth can look very different.

Some teeth are long and orange.
What animal is this?

This animal is a beaver. It uses its teeth to chew wood.

Some teeth are sharp and curved.
What animal is this?

This animal is a tiger. It uses its teeth
to catch and eat animals.

Some teeth are shaped like triangles.
What animal is this?

This animal is a shark. It uses its teeth to bite its food.

Some teeth are very thick.
What animal is this?

This animal is a hippopotamus.
It uses its teeth to crush food.

Some teeth are long and pointed.
What animal is this?

This animal is a narwhal. One of its teeth looks like a long horn!

Your Body

Do you have teeth?

Yes! Humans have teeth.

Humans use their teeth to chew food.

Can You Remember?

Which animal uses its teeth to chew wood?

Picture Glossary

 **horn** hard, bony body part that grows from an animal's head

 **teeth** hard body parts used for biting and chewing

Index

Notes for Parents and Teachers

Before reading

Create a KWL chart about teeth. On chart paper, make three columns and label them: "K - What do you know?", "W - What do you want to know?", and "L - What did you learn?". Ask the children what they know about teeth and fill in the K column of the chart together. Complete the W section of the chart on what they would like to know about teeth.

After reading

- Fill out the remaining section of the KWL chart with the children. Were there things that the children wanted to know about teeth which were not covered in the book? How could they find out about these things? Discuss the importance of finding information that is accurate.
- Display pictures of a number of different animals with different diets (e.g. cat, rabbit, shark, robin, horse). Ask the children if all these animals eat the same food. Then, display pictures of the food these animals eat (mice/small birds, lettuce/seeds, seals/fish, worms/grubs and grass/hay). Ask the children to link the animals to their diet. Discuss why they think these animals need different types of teeth to eat their food.